Birthday Cou...

Claire Amato

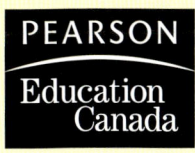

Toronto

Hooray! It is the month of October.
My birthday is in October.
I have been waiting all year for this day.

This year, I want to have a party.
I need to start counting the days and weeks.
I will use a calendar to start my birthday countdown.
I have many things to plan before my party.

Today is October 2.
My birthday is on October 30.
How many days are there until my birthday?

October

SUNDAY	MONDAY	TUESDAY	WEDNESDAY	THURSDAY	FRIDAY	SATURDAY
						1
2	3	4	5	6	7	8
9	10	11	12	13	14	15
16	17	18	19	20	21	22
23	24	25	26	27	28	29
30	31					

$$30 - 2 = 28$$

There are 28 days until my birthday.
I cannot wait that long!
How many school days are there until my birthday?

October

SUNDAY	MONDAY	TUESDAY	WEDNESDAY	THURSDAY	FRIDAY	SATURDAY
						1
(2)	3	4	5	6	7	8
9	10	11	12	13	14	15
16	17	18	19	20	21	22
23	24	25	26	27	28	29
(30)	31					

$5 + 5 + 5 + 5 = 20$

There are 20 school days until my birthday.
It still seems like a long time to wait.
How many weekends are there until my birthday?

OCTOBER

SUNDAY	MONDAY	TUESDAY	WEDNESDAY	THURSDAY	FRIDAY	SATURDAY
						1
2	3	4	5	6	7	8
9	10	11	12	13	14	15
16	17	18	19	20	21	22
23	24	25	26	27	28	29
30	31					

$1 + 1 + 1 + 1 = 4$

4 groups of 1 = 4

There are four weekends, or eight Saturdays and Sundays, until my birthday.
I do not have much time!
I should start writing my party invitations.
How many weeks are there until my birthday?

OCTOBER

SUNDAY	MONDAY	TUESDAY	WEDNESDAY	THURSDAY	FRIDAY	SATURDAY
						1
2	3	4	5	6	7	8
9	10	11	12	13	14	15
16	17	18	19	20	21	22
23	24	25	26	27	28	29
30	31					

There are seven days in a week.

There are four groups of seven.

So, there are four weeks.

There are only four weeks until my birthday.
I should start buying things for my party.
How many months are there until my birthday?

October

SUNDAY	MONDAY	TUESDAY	WEDNESDAY	THURSDAY	FRIDAY	SATURDAY
						1
(2)	3	4	5	6	7	8
9	10	11	12	13	14	15
16	17	18	19	20	21	22
23	24	25	26	27	28	29
(30)	31					

There is less than one month until my birthday. I do not have long to wait at all!

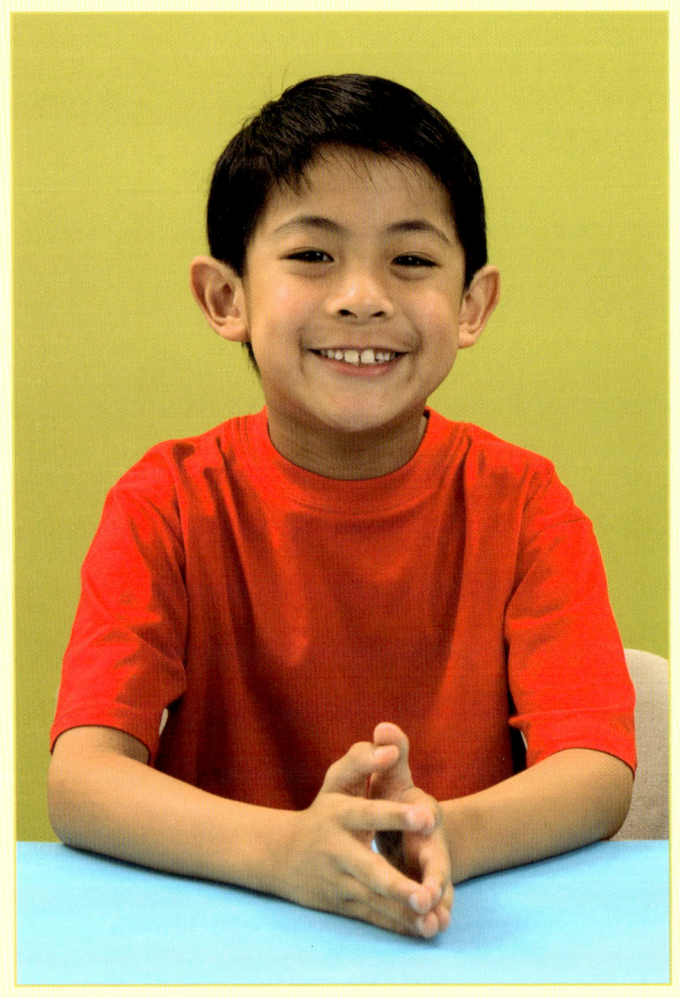

Now, I wonder how long I have to wait until my birthday next year.